JUDAISM

Myer Domnitz

The Bookwright Press
New York · 1986

Religions of the World

Buddhism
Christianity
Hinduism
Judaism

First published in the United States in 1986 by
The Bookwright Press
387 Park Avenue South
New York, NY 10016

First published in 1986 by
Wayland (Publishers) Limited
61 Western Road, Hove
East Sussex BN3 1JD, England

© Copyright 1986 Wayland (Publishers) Limited

ISBN 0-531-18066-2

Library of Congress Catalog Card Number: 85-73668

Phototypeset by Planagraphic Typesetters Limited
Printed and bound in Italy by Sagdos S.p.A.

Contents

Jews and Jewish History

Who are the Jews? There are Jews in many countries. They speak different languages and may be of any color. Anyone can become a Jew who believes in the Jewish religion, and obeys its laws and traditions according to the religious authorities. Anybody whose mother is a Jewess is also considered to be Jewish, even if he or she is not religious.

The Pharaoh agreed to free the Israelites from slavery.

The Israelites leaving Egypt.

Jewish history began over four thousand years ago in the Middle East. At that time, people worshiped many gods. According to the story in the Bible, a man named Abraham decided this was wrong and that there was only *one true God*.

God told Abraham and his family to leave their home in Mesopotamia and move to a place called Canaan. (Canaan was later called Israel and also Palestine.) God made a covenant, or agreement, with Abraham. He promised that Abraham and his descendants would become a great nation in Canaan, if they worshiped God and obeyed his laws. This is why Jews believe they have been chosen to make God known to the world.

Abraham and his family were called the Hebrews, from the word "Eber" meaning "from the other side." This was because they had come from the other side of the Euphrates River. Abraham had a son called Isaac, and a grandson called Jacob. Jacob later became known as Israel, or "Champion of God." Jacob had twelve sons whose descendants became the twelve tribes of Israel.

Many years later, the Hebrews left Canaan because of famine. They moved to Egypt because there was food there, but were later forced into slavery.

Moses, the adopted son of an Egyptian princess, was called by God to rescue his people, the Hebrews, from slavery. He told Pharaoh (the King of Egypt) that the Hebrews must be set free, or God would bring disaster to the land. Pharaoh did not agree to release the Hebrews until a series of plagues forced him to change his mind.

5

Moses led the Hebrews to freedom in the Sinai desert, and at the foot of Mount Sinai they heard God proclaim the Ten Commandments. Moses then set off alone to climb Mount Sinai, to receive instructions for the Hebrews from God. He returned after forty days with two stone tablets, on which were engraved the Ten Commandments. These were a set of rules for the Hebrews to live by, and in return God promised to look after them. In order to have a center for their religious ceremonies, Moses set up a tent called the Tabernacle in the wilderness. In it was the Ark of the Covenant, where the stone tablets inscribed with the Ten Commandments were kept.

The twelve tribes lived in the wilderness for the next forty years, becoming a nation called the Israelites.

Moses descended from Mount Sinai with the Ten Commandments.

The Israelites

Moses' successor was Joshua, and he led the Israelites back into Canaan. They were ruled by a succession of judges, prophets and kings. Among these early prophets was Samuel, who at God's command anointed Saul as the first King of the Israelites. However, Saul disobeyed God's commands and so he was replaced by the young shepherd, David. King David successfully fought the Israelites' warring neighbors and extended the kingdom. He captured the City of Jerusalem, and took the Ark of the Covenant there. Jerusalem became the center of worship in the Kingdom.

David is also remembered for his great religious poems — the psalms. These are still used today by Jews and Christians.

King David's psalms are still sung today.

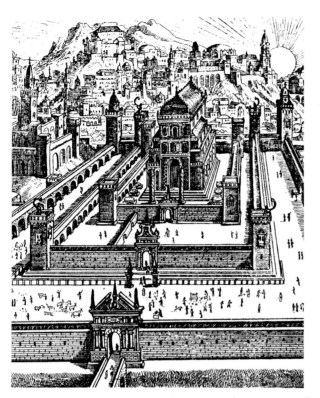

Solomon's Temple in Jerusalem.

David's son, Solomon, was the next king. He built a great temple in Jerusalem to house the Ark of the Covenant. But the rule of Solomon led to discontent, and when he died, the Israelite kingdom broke up. Ten tribes formed the kingdom of Israel and the remaining two tribes formed the kingdom of Judea.

The Israelites did not keep their covenant with God, and failed to live by the Ten Commandments. Prophets, or teachers, such as Elijah and Isaiah preached strongly against this, and tried to turn the Israelites back to their faith. But about 2,700 years ago, Israel was invaded by the Assyrians, and the people were taken off into captivity.

The kingdom of Israel was no more, and the ten tribes merged with their captors. Judea survived for another 125 years, until it was overrun by the Babylonians. Many of the people were taken to Babylon, and the Temple in Jerusalem was destroyed. But the people of Judea, or Jews as they became known, kept their faith alive and managed to strengthen it during their captivity.

Fifty years later, Babylon fell to the Persians, and the Jews were allowed to return to their country, now called Palestine. They rebuilt the Temple in Jerusalem.

About 1,900 years ago, Palestine was invaded by the Romans and the Temple was destroyed. Many Jews fled to other countries. Those who settled in northern, central and eastern Europe were called Ashkenazim, while those who settled in Spain, Portugal and North Africa were called Sephardim. Over the following centuries, Jewish communities were established all over the world.

Jews were often savagely persecuted because of their religion. Most hoped that one day they would be able to return to the Promised Land, but this was not to happen until the twentieth century. In 1948, the State of Israel was set up as an independent Jewish state. Jews came to settle there from all over the world. Many other Jews supported Israel, but remained as citizens in the countries where they had long been established and made many contributions to national life.

Basic Beliefs

Jews believe there is one God, who is everlasting. Jews also believe they have a special duty to make God's holy teachings known to all people: this can be shown by the way they live their lives.

Jews do not believe in the divinity of Christ. They believe there will be a Messiah in the future, who will unite all people under God's command, bringing lasting peace. Because Jews do not believe in the divinity of Jesus Christ, they do not use the terms BC (before Christ) and AD (in the year of the Lord). Instead they use the abbreviations BCE (before the Common Era: before year I) and CE (Common Era: after the year I). The Jewish Messiah will be God's messenger of peace, but he will be a human being, unlike Jesus, who in Christian teachings was the son of God and a redeemer. In Judaism, no one comes between God and his creatures. Redemption is only possible through God, when real repentance is achieved through good deeds.

Loving God also means loving your neighbor. Jewish people provide charitable help for their own people and those of other faiths. The rabbis teach that charitable work must be carried out in a spirit of understanding and compassion.

When dealing with other people, the Jewish scriptures, the *Torah* and *Talmud,* set out high standards of

A student receiving religious instruction from a Rabbi.

conduct. Rights and duties of workers and employers were laid down. Wages were fixed to safeguard standards of living, and had to be paid promptly. Fundamental human rights such as liberty, freedom and equality were demanded, which related to the prophets' strong condemnation of injustice.

Judaism teaches that there is life after death.

9

Holy Books — The Torah and Talmud

The *Torah* (teaching) contains the first five books of the Bible, which tell of the covenants God made with Abraham, Isaac and Jacob. It sets out the Ten Commandments revealed by God to Moses after the covenant at Mount Sinai, laws and practices to guard basic human rights, and the duties of a Jew. The *Torah* also explained how the Israelites were to be trained to carry out God's teachings.

The *Talmud* (to study) is a written collection of interpretations of the Bible and instructions on the Jewish way of life. It is based on oral teachings from the time of Moses.

Orthodox Jews praying at the Western Wall.

These teachings were brought together and explained by Rabbi Akivah (50-135 CE) then written down and organized by Judah the Prince (135-217 CE), and are known as the *Mishnah* (repetition). Judah was considered the main authority on these teachings. *The Mishnah* is written in Hebrew and is divided into six main subject areas for study. These are arranged into sixty-three volumes covering the main aspects of religious law in Jewish life.

The *Gemara* (completion) is a series of discussions and commentaries on the *Mishnah*. The *Gemara* and *Mishnah* together make up the *Talmud*.

The *Talmud* is studied in colleges by those who wish to become rabbis and teachers. Synagogues also hold regular sessions for the study of the *Talmud* by their members.

Different Forms of Judaism

There have been different forms of Judaism since the earliest times. Today, these different movements can be grouped under three main headings — Orthodox, Conservative and Reform. Orthodox Jews believe that the Jewish laws and teachings of the *Torah* must be followed today exactly as they were laid down in the time of Moses and developed in the *Talmud*. Non-Orthodox Jews believe that some of the *Torah's* teachings can be adapted to make them more relevant to life in the modern world.

Reform Judaism first developed in Germany during the first half of the nineteenth century. It moved away from the Orthodox view of the Hebrew Bible and the *Talmud*. In the second half of the nineteenth century, the United States became the center of the movement when the Reform leader emigrated here from Germany. Reform Jews gave up many of the ritual practices and ceremonies that are essential to Orthodox Judaism.

Conservative Jews broke away from the Reform movement to become more traditional, so their beliefs fall halfway between Orthodox and Reform Judaism.

Orthodox and non-Orthodox Jews have different ways of worshiping at the Jewish place of worship, the synagogue. In an Orthodox synagogue,

Orthodox Jews in the Old City of Jerusalem.

men and women must worship separately, following the ancient traditions of the Temple in Jerusalem. In non-Orthodox synagogues, men and women sit together. Women play only a small part in the religious life at Orthodox synagogues, but at Conservative and Reform synagogues they take a more equal part with men. Orthodox Jews do not permit women to become rabbis, but non-Orthodox Jews do. The language used to conduct the service also differs. Orthodox Jews all over the world use Hebrew for their service, with a translation in the local language in the prayer book. Non-Orthodox Jews use both Hebrew and their own language.

A popular movement among Jews in

Eastern Europe was the Hasidic. This was established in the eighteenth century by Israel Baal Sham Tov (Master of a Good Name). He taught that contact with God is achieved through prayer in a state of happiness and emphasized love of human beings. A group within the Hasidic movement known as the Lubavich has become especially popular with the young throughout the world.

Today there is an important group of Hasadim in Brooklyn, in New York,

An Orthodox synagogue in Jerusalem.

where the Lubavich Rabbinical College has been established. They are a very close-knit community, and hold to the old ways, wearing traditional clothing and hairstyles.

As in most religions, there are also many non-observant individuals — people who consider themselves Jewish but do not obey Jewish religious laws or attend services in a synagogue.

12

The Synagogue

The synagogue is a house of prayer and study and a community center. Synagogues first came into being during the time of the Babylonian exile under the leadership of the prophet Ezekiel. Synagogues were places for the Jews to meet and keep their faith alive. When they returned to the Holy Land, the people built synagogues there. The Hebrew word for synagogue is *Beth Ha — Knesset,* meaning house of meeting or assembly. (*Knesset* is also the name given to the Israeli Parliament today.) When the Temple in Jerusalem was destroyed by the Romans, synagogues became the places of worship for all Jewish communities.

A modern European synagogue.

The Ark

The central feature of the synagogue is the Ark, which houses the scrolls of the *Torah*. It is placed against the eastern wall facing Jerusalem. Above the Ark are models of the two stone tablets of the Ten Commandments, which Moses brought down from Mount Sinai. The parchment scrolls of the *Torah* are written in Hebrew, which is read from right to left. They are prepared by highly skilled scribes who use quill pens, according to tradition.

There is an embroidered curtain hanging in front of the Ark, recalling the veil or cover near the Ark in the Tabernacle. A light called the *Ner Tamid* is always kept burning in front of the Ark. This acts as a reminder of the golden seven-branched candelabrum, the *menorah,* which burned in the Tabernacle and the Temple in Jerusalem.

The Torah *scrolls are kept in the synagogue Ark.*

The Torah being taken from the Ark.

15

The Torah *scrolls being carried to the reading desk.*

There is a raised platform in the center of the synagogue, with a reading desk or table from which the cantor (prayer leader) leads the congregation in worship. The scrolls of the *Torah* are placed on the desk for readings on the Sabbath, on festivals and on Monday and Thursday mornings. The bells of the crown on top of the scrolls make a pleasant sound as they are carried through the synagogue to be placed on the reading desk. The crown, together with the velvet covering mantle, is removed and the scroll is stretched on the reading desk. Its parchment is joined by wooden rollers known as the Tree of Life, or *Etz Hayim*. Scrolls are often decorated with a breastplate worn by the High Priest at services in the Temple in Jerusalem. It is decorated with twelve precious stones to represent the twelve tribes of Israel.

The services

Orthadox Jews have three prayer sessions each day, at the synagogue, at home or anywhere else. For a synagogue service a minimum of ten men, called a *minyan*, must be present.

During the service, members of the congregation are called upon to read the *Torah*. The first to be called are people with the surname Cohen, descendants of the priests, or *Cohanim*, of the First Temple in Jerusalem. They are followed by the descendants of the

The breastplate on the Torah *scroll.*

17

Levites, *Levys,* and finally members of the general congregation. The reader of the *Torah* uses a special chant. He has a finger-shaped pointer, called a *yad,* to keep his place on the scroll. After the

A pointer is used to read from the Torah.

reading from the scroll, there are readings from the prophets and prayers.

A reminder of the importance of synagogue services are the words in Hebrew above the Ark meaning "Know before whom you stand," and "Happy are they that dwell in Thy House, they will be forever praising Thee."

Being Jewish

We have already seen that Jews who settled in different parts of the world can be divided into two main groups: the Ashkenazim and the Sephardim. (In general, the Ashkenazim settled in Christian countries and the Sephardim in Muslim countries.) The two groups share the same beliefs, but many differ in their ways of worship and customs.

Language

Hebrew has always been used for worship and is the popular language of Israel today. The Ashkenazim and the Sephardim each have their own languages for everyday use. The Ashkenazim speak *Yiddish,* a mixture of Hebrew and medieval German, and the Sephardim speak *Ladino,* a mixture of Hebrew and medieval Spanish. Both *Yiddish* and *Ladino* are written in Hebrew letters. Jews continue to speak *Yiddish* in Europe and America, but *Ladino* is very rare. The Jews of Ethiopia, the Falashas, have their own language.

Falashas, black Ethiopian Jews, holding a holy book.

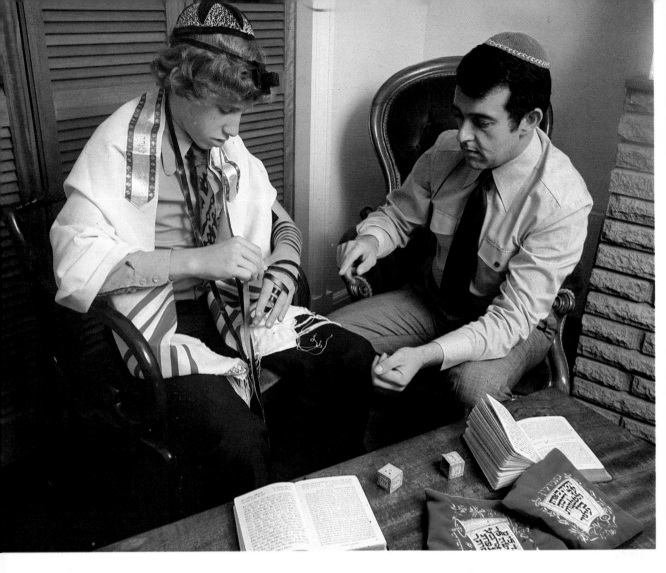

Signs

It is customary for Orthodox Jewish men to wear a skullcap called a *yarmulke* or *kippah* at all times. The men also wear a prayer shawl, or *tallit*, for prayers. The fringes at the ends of the shawl are a reminder to carry out the Lord's commandments and to be holy unto God.

Orthodox Jewish men also wear phylacteries, or *tefillin* for their weekday morning prayers. These phylacteries are

A young boy learning to put on a tefillin *prior to his* Bar Mitzvah.

small leather boxes containing Biblical texts written on parchment. They are worn on the forehead, to be close to the mind, and on the left upper arm, to be facing the heart. This expresses the Jewish prayer called the *Shema*, which says that God's wishes should be carried out with all one's being. Phylacteries are worn by boys from the age of thirteen, when they become *Bar-Mitzvah* (see page 23).

Food laws

Orthodox Jews have strict rules about diet. Only animals that chew the cud and have cloven hoofs, such as cows and sheep, may be eaten. Thus pigs and rabbits are forbidden. Fish that have scales and fins are allowed, but not shellfish or eels.

For Orthodox Jews, there are laws about the preparation of food, too. Blood must not be eaten, so animals are killed in such a way that all the blood drains out of the body. This is carried out by highly-trained people who see to it that the animals feel no pain. Food prepared according to Orthodox Jewish law is called *kosher*.

Orthodox Jews may not eat milk and meat products together. Separate sets of untensils are kept for cooking meat and dairy dishes. Strict Jews wait for several hours after eating a meat dish before eating a milk product.

Symbols

Outside Orthodox Jewish homes you will see a small box attached to the right-hand doorpost, called a *mezzuzah*. The *mezzuzah* contains a parchment scroll

The seven-branched menorah *in a stained-glass window.*

with paragraphs from the *Shema,* a Jewish prayer, written on it. It is a continual sign of God's connection with the home. *Mezzuzahs* are also found on other doorposts inside the house.

One of the oldest Jewish symbols is the candelabra known as the *menorah.* The original *menorah* was made of gold and was kept in the Tabernacle, and later the Temple. Today the *menorah* is the official symbol of Israel.

The Star of David.

The Star of David is another well-known Jewish symbol. It is made up of two intertwined triangles, and represents the shield used by King David. In Hebrew it is called the *Magen David.* A further meaning is that the six sides at the center of the triangles represent the Sabbath, and the six corners stand for the six working days.

22

Religious Rites

Growing Up

Jews have both a Hebrew name and an ordinary name. The Hebrew name is used in the synagogue and on religious documents. A baby boy is given his name when he is eight days old, after a circumcision ceremony. In the Bible it states that God said to Abraham, "you and your descendants shall keep my covenant." The covenant was marked by the circumcision of all males. Abraham circumcised his son Isaac when he was eight days old. This became the usual age for the circumcision of baby boys. Baby girls are named with the saying of a special prayer at the synagogue.

When boys are thirteen, they are considered to be adults and become responsible for their religious duties. This is marked with a ceremony called *Bar Mitzvah,* meaning "Son of the Commandment." The ceremony takes place at the synagogue on the Sabbath nearest to the boy's birthday. Girls are confirmed at twelve, and some non-Orthodox synagogues hold a special service called *Bat Mitzvah,* when the girl becomes a "Daughter of the Commandment." A girl prepares for this by learn-

A Bar Mitzvah *at the Western Wall, Jerusalem.*

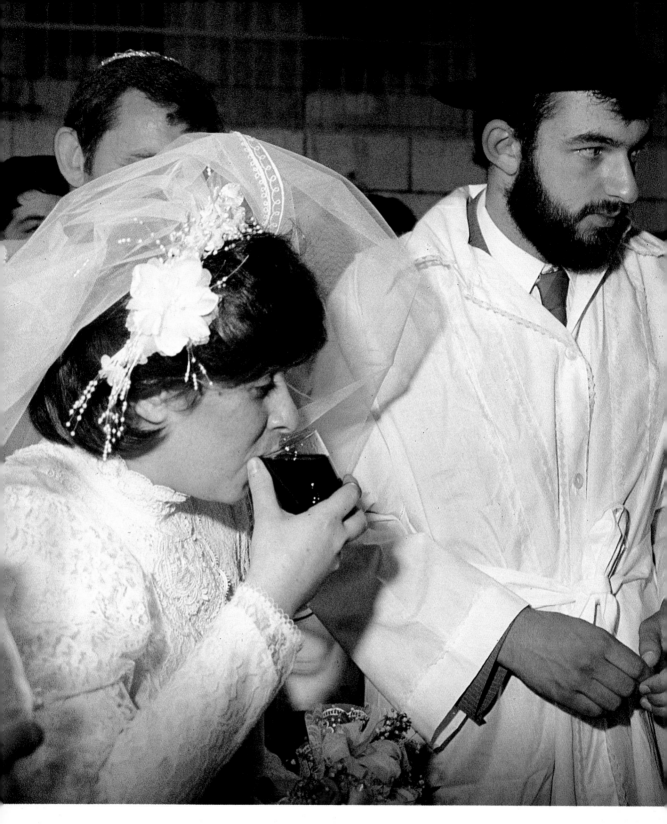

An Orthodox Jewish wedding ceremony.

ing about her future role as a wife and mother.

Many Jewish children attend classes to study Judaism. Boys must learn Hebrew, so they can read the Hebrew prayers in the synagogue. A boy will have to read from the *Torah* at his *Bar Mitzvah*.

Marriage

Marriage is very important in Judaism. It is considered to be a holy institution, as shown by the Hebrew word for the ceremony, *kiddushin,* meaning "made holy." In a traditional ceremony the groom signs a marriage document, the *ketubah,* in which he undertakes to be a true husband, to honor, cherish and support his wife. At the ceremony, the bride and groom stand under an embroidered canopy called a *chuppah,* which represents their future home. An address is given by the rabbi, and the cantor says the betrothal blessing over a glass of wine, from which the couple sip in turn. The couple make their vows and other blessings are recited. At the end of the service, the bridegroom breaks a glass under his foot to symbolize the destruction of the Temple, and as a reminder that there will be bad times as well as good in the marriage.

Later on this happy day, there is a celebration dinner for family and friends. Hebrew songs are sung, and the day winds up with dancing, especially of the well-known Israeli dance, called

A Jewish wedding contract.

Hora, with its cheerful refrain *"Hava Negila"* — "Come, sing and be happy."

Death

Jewish burials usually take place within two days of the death. Orthodox Jews do

25

not allow cremation, but non-Orthodox Jews do. At the cemetery, the dead person's son and other close relatives say a moving prayer called the *Kaddish,* which expresses the hope that God's Kingdom will be established on earth.

Orthodox families are in mourning at home for seven days after the funeral, and friends come to comfort them. Prayers are recited at home during this period. For the next eleven months, the sons and closest relative say the *Kaddish* every day if they are Orthodox, or every Sabbath if they are non-Orthodox. The *Kaddish* continues to be said annually, on the anniversary of their relative's death.

A mourner reciting the Kaddish *memorial prayer at a funeral.*

The Sabbath

Especially in the case of Orthodox Jews, the Sabbath *(Shabbat),* is a special "day of delight" after the working week. It begins shortly after sunset on Friday evening and ends late on Saturday night. As the seventh day of the week, the Sabbath is a day of rest, to be spent at home with the family. No work may be done on the Sabbath, so all the preparation, such as buying food and cooking, must be done beforehand.

At home the mother marks the start of the Sabbath by lighting candles and saying a blessing over them. The whole family usually visits the synagogue in the evening. When they return home, everybody sits down for a special meal together. The meal begins with a blessing said by the father called *kiddush.* He also blesses his children and gives thanks for his wife. A blessing is said over two specially-baked braided loaves called *challah,* eaten as a reminder that God provided a double portion of manna (food) for the Israelites in the wilderness. Happy songs called *zemiroth* are sung during the meal.

There are services at the synagogue on the morning and afternoon of the Sabbath. In the afternoon, the family may attend a study session at the synagogue, stay at home or visit friends. At the end of the Sabbath, there is a ceremony called *havdalah* to show the difference between the holiness of the

The Mother marks the start of the Sabbath by lighting candles and saying a prayer.

Specially baked and braided loaves are eaten on the Sabbath.

Sabbath and weekdays. A blessing is said over wine and a lighted candle. A spice box containing sweet-smelling spices is blessed. It stands for the sweetness of the Sabbath and the hope that this will continue through the week. A blessing is said over the candle to mark the approach of the new week, and as a reminder that God created light on the first day.

The Father blesses the Sabbath wine at the beginning of the meal.

Jewish Festivals

Passover

Passover celebrates the Exodus of the Israelites from Egypt. The festival lasts eight days in late March or early April. On the first two nights, there is a celebration called *seder,* when family and friends gather for a special meal, during which a book called the *Haggadah* is read and sung aloud. It tells the story of the Exodus. The youngest person present asks four questions starting "Why is this night different from all other nights?," and these are answered in the *Haggadah.*

The Havdalah *ceremony marks the end of the Sabbath.*

*Family and friends gather for a
special meal at* Seder.

During Passover, only unleavened
bread called *matzoth* is eaten. This is a
reminder of the time the Israelites
escaped from slavery in Egypt. They left
in such a hurry that there was no time

for the dough to rise; so they had to eat
unleavened bread.

The seder meal contains various other
foods that symbolize the harsh treatment of the children of Israel. There are
bitter herbs to represent the bitterness of
slavery. A mixture of apples, almonds,
raisins, cinnamon and wine symbolizes

the mortar used by the slaves in building for their masters.

The table is set with a special glass of wine, known as Elijah's glass, with the hope that the prophet will return to the world to herald the arrival of the Messiah. Many songs are sung, making *seder* especially popular with children as a happy occasion. The message of Passover is to look to the future under God's guidance.

Blessing the Seder *wine.*

Shavuot

Shavuot takes place seven weeks after Passover and celebrates the *receiving* of the Ten Commandments at Mount Sinai. In ancient times, Jews would set aside some barley during Passover. After seven weeks, the barley was ready to be harvested and was brought to Jerusalem as an offering. At *Shavuot,* synagogues are adorned with fragrant flowers and plants, to remind the congregation of pilgrims taking their first fruits to the Temple.

Synagogues are decorated with flowers at Shavuot.

Sukkoth

The autumn festival of *Sukkoth,* or Tabernacles, reminds Jews of the life of the Israelites during their forty years in the wilderness. They lived in huts called *sukkoth,* so for this festival, Jewish families put up *sukkoth* in their gardens or yards. A *succah,* or booth, has a roof of branches, from which fruit and flowers are hung. Children are anxious to make their *succah* as attractive as possible with many decorations. The family have their meals there, and spend as much time in it as possible.

A sukkoth *being erected.*

33

A sukkoth *festival at the Western Wall, Jerusalem.*

During the morning synagogue service, people hold myrtle, willow and palm branches in their right hands, and a citrus fruit called etrog in their left. Etrog is the symbol of the heart, palm of the spinal cord, myrtle of the eye, and willow of the lips. These symbolize the worship of God with all one's being, and the plants are waved in all directions to show that God is everywhere.

The ninth and last day of the festival is called *Simchat Torah,* the Rejoicing

Scrolls are carried round in the Rejoicing of the Torah.

of the *Torah.* The last chapter of the *Torah* is read, followed by the first chapter. This shows that the reading of the *Torah* never ceases and a new cycle of readings begins. This is a joyful time when children carry banners and sing cheerful hymns with the adults, who carry the *Torah* scrolls around the synagogue.

35

Rosh Hashanah

Rosh Hashanah is the first day of the Jewish New Year, and takes place in September or October. It celebrates the Creation, but is also a day of judgement, when God desires the return to the Faith of all who have strayed. God is described as Judge of the world, weighing up the future of human beings.

During the synagogue service, a *shofar* (curved ram's horn) is blown as an urgent call to everyone to return to God and His worship.

At *Rosh Hashanah,* it is the custom at home to eat pieces of apple dipped in honey, to express the wish for a pleasant and sweet New Year.

Blowing the shofar *on the Jewish New Year.*

Yom Kippur

During the days following *Rosh Hashanah,* according to Orthodox tradition, God decides whether bad deeds should be punished. These days are known as the Ten Days of Penitence, when Jews pray for forgiveness for their sins. The tenth day is *Yom Kippur,* or Day of Atonement.

Most Orthodox men spend the day in the synagogue. White robes may be worn to suggest purity and hope. Fasting begins at sunset on the previous evening, continuing until nightfall on *Yom Kippur.* The opening prayer of the fast is called *Kol Nidrei,* meaning "all vows." This seeks pardon for vows made to the Almighty, but not kept. It urges all those who have strayed, sometimes under compulsion, to return to their faith on this most solemn day. Promises made to people can only be broken by mutual consent. In the final service, called *Neilah,* hope is expressed that worshipers will be forgiven by the Almighty, and granted a happy life in the future. The blowing of the *shofar* marks the end of the fast, and symbolizes a challenge to keep to God's worship during the coming year.

Chanukkah

This winter festival celebrates an event that happened over 2,000 years ago. A small Jewish army, led by the heroic

A candle is lit for every day of the Chanukkah *festival.*

Judah the Macabee, defeated the powerful Syrian army, which had invaded the Holy Land and occupied Jerusalem. When the Jews regained the Temple in Jerusalem they found it had been defiled with idols. They cleansed and rededicated the Temple to the worship of God, but could only find a small jar of oil to light the *menorah.* Instead of burning for one day, as expected, the oil miraculously lasted for eight days.

So the festival of *Chanukkah* is celebrated by lighting a candle on the first night and adding an extra one on each of the following seven nights.

Purim

The story of the spring festival of *Purim* is described in the Book of Esther in the Bible. It tells how through God's help, Esther saved the Jews from destruction by an evil man named Haman. During the synagogue service, the story is read out. Every time the name of Haman, the villain, is spoken, all the children hiss and rattle special noisemakers called *groggers*.

Children perform plays and dress up as characters from the story of Esther. In Tel Aviv, the *Purim* Carnival is a popular event, which attracts many visitors.

Purim *carnival in Israel.*

Anti-Semitism

Anti-semitism in its deepest form means hatred of Jews. Some of the blame for this lies in an interpretation of the Gospels, which holds Jews responsible for the crucifixion of Jesus. It should be remembered that *Jesus was a Jew* and that his teachings on loving one's neighbors were first stated in the Old Testament — the Hebrew Bible.

For centuries Jews were forced to live in special areas of towns called ghettos, separated from their Christian neighbors. This led to continuing misunderstanding and hatred. Whole Jewish communities were wiped out in the Middle Ages because they refused to give up their faith.

During World War II, Adolf Hitler and his Nazi followers built on long established Christian anti-Semitism to bring about the deaths of over six million innocent Jewish men, women and children. There are many moving accounts of bravery and self-sacrifice from this time. One such story concerns Dr. Janus Korczak, the director of the Warsaw Jewish Orphanage. Despite Nazi offers of freedom, he went with the children from his orphanage to the death camp at Treblinka — he could never forsake them. The survival of Jews in Europe can only be seen as a miracle.

After these terrible events world Church leaders strongly condemned Christian anti-Semitism. They recognized it as a major factor in the Nazi

Jewish families were sent to their deaths by the Nazis.

plan for the mass destruction of millions of human beings.

Even today, Jews suffer for their faith. In the Soviet Union, prayer books and Bibles are very hard to get, and the teaching of Hebrew and Judaism is forbidden. Jewish teachers are harassed and sent to prison on trumped-up charges. Yet many young people have a strong urge to follow their family faith, and take risks to learn about it. Many Jews have applied to be allowed to go to Israel. They are known as "refuseniks," as they are usually refused permission. They then often lose their jobs, and their children are harassed at school. There has been a sharp drop in the number of Jews allowed to leave the Soviet Union for Israel. The lowest total, of around 900, was in 1984.

Jews of the World

Today, the world population of Jews is estimated at about 17 million, and is scattered all over the globe. About 3,000,000 Jews live in Israel, and nearly twice that number in the United States.

United States

The Jewish community in the United States numbers over 6 million and is the largest in the world. New York has about 2 million Jews among its population.

The first Jewish settlers arrived in New Amsterdam in the seventeenth century. Among the earliest to come were Sephardic Jews from Spain. They were followed over the years by many Jews from Europe who came to America in order to escape persecution and lead a freer life. The United States Constitution was in fact the first to guarantee religious freedom to every citizen.

The oldest existing synagogue in the United States is the Touro synagogue in Newport, Rhode Island. It was built in 1763 and is now a national historic site. Wooden pegs were used instead of nails in building it, and under the reader's

The Bevis Mark synagogue is the oldest in Britain.

desk there is a door to a secret passage, which once led to the street. Even in America, Jews did not always feel safe from persecution.

Although but a small part of the population (about 3%), Jews have played an important role in this country. Partly because of traditional Jewish emphasis on education and scholarship, Jews have risen to the top in many fields. Justice Louis Brandeis was the first Jew to be appointed to the United States Supreme Court, and was known for his sense of social justice based on the teachings of the Hebrew prophets. Jonas Salk prepared the first vaccine against polio. Leonard Bernstein is among the

Elderly members being served tea by volunteers of a Jewish Welfare Board.

best-known modern composers. Barbara Tuchman is an eminent historian.

This list could be extended to include many other Jews in fields such as entertainment, athletics, and journalism. In politics, there are Jewish mayors and governors, and many members of Congress and the cabinet. In fact about the only high position in the United States not yet held by a Jew is the presidency.

Many Jews emigrated to the United States to lead a freer life.

42

Britain

The Jewish community in Britain goes back to 1656. Today it numbers about 333,000. Most of the synagogues are Orthodox. The oldest synagogue was established in London in 1701.

Among the 37,000 Jewish refugees who went to Britain to escape from the Nazi terror were many distinguished scholars in different fields. Among those honored for outstanding research was Sir Ernest Chain, a leading bio-chemist, who shared the Nobel Prize for Medicine for his work on penicillin, and Sir Ludwig Guttman, founder of a hospital for the treatment of spinal injuries. In the world of music, Yehudi Menhuin, the famous violinist, founded a school to encourage youthful music talent. And in all other fields as well, Jewish citizens in Britain are active in national and local life.

These stained-glass windows were designed by the famous French artist Marc Chagall.

France

The Jewish community in France has a history over 1,000 years old. Among its great Jewish scholars in the Middle Ages was a Rabbi Solomon son of Isaac (1040-1105), popularly known as Rashi, his initials in Hebrew. His explanations of the *Torah* and *Talmud* teachings have been part of religious learning for generations, and are still used in many countries.

French Jews were freed from hard restrictions in 1791 during the Revolution. Many Jews came to France from Russia at the end of the nineteenth century. Tragically, 120,000 French Jews were deported or massacred during the Nazi occupation of France during World War II. After the war, the Jewish community grew to about 600,000 — the largest in Western Europe, swelled by refugees from North Africa.

There are well known Jews in many areas of French life, one of the most famous being Marc Chagall, the artist.

U.S.S.R. and Poland

There have been Jewish communities in Russia and Poland for over 1,000 years. After 1917, the Soviet Government made many harsh regulations against its Jews. It is estimated that there are about 2½ million Jews now in the U.S.S.R.

The Nazi invasion of Poland during World War II led to the destruction of 3 million Jews, and now there are only about 8,000 left.

The loss of Jewish learning centers in Russia and Poland greatly affected Jewish communities all over the world.

Israel has transformed its desert wilderness into rich farmland.

Israel

We now return to the Promised Land of Israel where our story began.

In the nineteenth century, a movement grew among Jews in many countries, who wanted to reestablish the Jewish homeland in Palestine. They were called Zionists after Mount Zion, which lies northeast of Jerusalem. These young pioneers drained the swamps that caused malaria and helped to plant trees since many had been destroyed over the centuries. In 1914, 85,000 Jews had their homes in Palestine.

In 1917 the British Government issued the Balfour Declaration, which supported the idea of a national

Israel today is a combination of the old and new.

homeland for the Jewish people. After World War I, Britain administered Palestine, and a steady stream of Jews began to settle there. It was hoped that there would be friendship and cooperation among the Jewish, Muslim and Christian communities. But this did not happen.

When the British administration of Palestine ended in 1947, the United Nations recommended that independent Jewish and Arab states should be established there. The Jewish leaders accepted this proposal, but the Arabs did not. The State of Israel was born in 1948. But fighting soon broke out be-

tween the Arabs and Israelis; over 700,000 Jews were expelled from Arab countries and welcomed in Israel. The first peace treaty between Israel and an Arab country was made with Egypt in 1979.

The population of Israel is now over 4 million: 83 percent are Jews. The rest are Muslims, Christians, Druse and people of other religions. All religious communities have freedom of worship and their own representatives in parliament. Between 1980 and 1985 thousands of Falashas, black Jews, were rescued from the famine stricken areas of Ethiopia and brought to Israel, their Promised Land.

Jews throughout the world have a close bond with Israel, and use a beautiful word to express their hope for a better future — *Shalom:* Peace!

45

Glossary

Anti-Semitism Hostility toward Jews, which may result in discrimination and persecution.

Ark In ancient times, the holy receptacle containing the tablets of the Ten Commandments. The Ark in a synagogue contains the scrolls of the *Torah*.

Ashkenazim Usually refers to Jews who settled in Christian countries.

Bar Mitzvah The ceremony at which a boy of thirteen is confirmed. *Bat Mitzvah* is the name of the ceremony for girls.

Cantor A prayer leader in the synagogue.

Circumcision The removal of the foreskin from the penis.

Covenant An agreement made by God with Abraham and Moses.

Challah Special braided loaves eaten on the Sabbath.

Crucifixion A Roman form of execution.

Kosher Food which has been prepared according to Jewish law.

Matzoth Unleavened bread which is eaten throughout Passover.

Menorah A seven-branched candelabrum. The original *Menorah* was kept burning continually in the Temple in Jerusalem.

Messiah The savior the Jews believe will one day come to the earth, bringing lasting peace.

Mezzuzah A small container holding parts of the prayer called the *Shema*. It is fixed to the doorposts of Jewish homes.

Orthodox Jews Jews who follow strictly the teachings of Moses.

Phylacteries Small leather boxes containing religious texts, worn on the forehead and left arm. Called *tefillin* in Hebrew.

Rabbi The chief official of a synagogue, who is a teacher and leader of students of the *Torah*.

Sephardim Usually refers to Jews who settled in Spain and Portugal.

Shema The most important Jewish prayer. It is the first learned by children and the last spoken by the dying.

Tabernacle A tent in which the Israelites placed the Ark of the Covenant.

Tallit A prayer shawl worn by Orthodox men.

Talmud The teachings and discussions of the oral laws of Moses made by the rabbis, and later compiled into written form.

Temple The Temple in Jerusalem built by King Solomon, which was the focal point for Jewish worship.

Ten Commandments The commandments of God, as revealed by Moses after going up Mount Sinai, which were a guide to how the Israelites should live.

Torah The first five books of the Bible.

Yiddish A language spoken by *Ashkenazim* Jews, based on Hebrew and medieval German.

Books to Read

Geffner, Anne. *A Child Celebrates: The Jewish Holidays, rev. ed.* Sepulveda, CA: Double M Press, 1980.

Golomb, Morris. *Know Jewish Living and Enjoy It.* New York: Shengold, 1981.

Greenberg, Judith E. and Helen Carey. *Jewish Holidays.* New York: Franklin Watts, 1985.

Keene, Michael. *Being a Jew.* North Pomfret, VT: David & Charles, 1985.

Kripke, Dorothy K. and Meyer Levin. *God and the Story of Judaism.* New York: Behrman House, 1962.

Rosenblum, Richard. *My Bar Mitzvah.* New York: Morrow, 1985.

Index

Picture Acknowledgments

The publishers would like to thank all those who provided the illustrations on the following pages: Camerapix Hutchison Library 11, 18, 26; JPMP 17, 19, 22, 40, 41, 44, 45; Mansell Collection 5, 6, 7, 8, 42; ZEFA *front cover, frontispiece,* 9, 10, 12, 13, 14, 15, 16, 20, 21, 23, 24, 25, 27 *(top),* 27 *(bottom),* 28, 29, 30, 31, 32, 33, 34, 35, 36, 37, 38, 43; Sobell House 41.